THE POWER OF THE CROSS

Steve Green

Darlene Chamberlin
1994

SPARROW

Sparrow Press
Nashville, Tennessee

Published 1994 in Nashville, Tennessee, by Sparrow Press, and distributed in Canada by Christian Marketing Canada, Ltd.

Printed in the United States of America

98 97 96 95 94   5 4 3 2 1

Library of Congress Cataloging-in-Publication Data

Green, Steve.
       A 30 day devotional on the power of the cross /
       Steve Green
           p.   cm.
       ISBN 0-917143-27-2 :
       1. Christian life—Meditations.
       2. Devotional calendars.
       3. Green, Steve. I. Title. II. Title: Power of
       the cross. III. Title: Thirty day
       devotional on the power of the cross.
       BV4501.2.G7453   1994
       242' .2—dc20
                                        93-43856
                                        CIP

Quotations and song lyrics in each chapter are from the following:
Ch.1: "Find Us Faithful" by Jon Mohr, © 1987 Birdwing Music (a div. of The Sparrow Corporation)/BMG Songs, Inc. and Jonathan Mark Music. All rights reserved. International copyright secured. Used by permission.
Ch.9: "Until Then" by Stuart Hamblen, ©1958 Hamblen Music Co., Inc. A.R.R./U.B.P.
Ch. 13: "The Mission" by Jon Mohr, © 1989 Feed & Seed Music and J.R. Dennis Music. All rights reserved. Used by Permission.
Ch.21: "Christ The Solid Rock" words by Edward Mote, Elma Hendrix, P.D.

Scripture quotations are from the New Revised Standard Version of the Bible, copyright 1989 by the Division of Christian Education of the National Council of the Churches of Christ in the USA. Used by permission. All rights reserved.

Compiled & edited by Deborah Harris
Cover design by Sara Remke
Book design by Mike Goodson

CONTENTS

INTRODUCTION

One of the consequences of the Fall is our loss of memory. All too easily I can forget important truths and need to be reminded of them again. Often, while listening to a sermon, a simple word deeply affects me. It is not that I have not heard it before. It is that I have forgotten it. Repeatedly, Scripture exhorts us to "remember" and "not forget." The apostle Peter wrote in his second letter, "I intend to keep on reminding you of these things, though you know them already and are established in the truth that has come to you. I think it is right, as long as I am in this body, to refresh your memory . . . " (2 Pet. 1:12–13).

We titled this collection *The Power of the Cross.* In addressing the Corinthian church, Paul said that although there were many noble themes and significant ideas, he wanted them to understand what was supremely important: "That Christ died for our sins according to the Scriptures, that he was buried, that he was raised on the third day according to the Scriptures, and that he appeared to Peter, and then to the Twelve"

(1 Cor. 15:3–5). This is the foundation of our faith and the hope for our daily living.

The thoughts in this book are not new, and others have expressed them more eloquently. But I pray that they will gently remind you and refresh you so that you will pursue Christ with increased passion.

1

THE POWER OF
THE CROSS

*For the message about the cross
is foolishness to those who
are perishing, but to us who are
being saved it is the power of God.*

1 Corinthians 1:18

People respond differently to the cross of
Christ. My friend Max Lucado observed that
some people idolize the cross, and some gold-
plate it. Others despise the cross and burn it.
One thing is certain—the cross cannot be
ignored. It stands stark against the backdrop
of history and eternity, with a message to all
humanity.

The cross speaks to us first of Jesus Christ.
My daughter's school dictionary defines Jesus
as the founder of the Christian religion, but he
is much more than that. He is God become
visible, the power of God incarnate. He is the
Father's most articulate expression, the Word
in human form. He infuriated the Pharisees
by declaring himself to be God, saying,
"Before Abraham was born, I Am." He told
his disciples that if they had seen him, they

had seen the Father. Statements like that cannot be disregarded. How will we respond to this Jesus?

The cross that Jesus died on also speaks to us of the power of sin to steal from us eternal life, and of God's judgment against sin. Sin is not only wrong *doing*, but wrong *being*—a state of spiritual separation from God. Historically, animal sacrifices served to remind Israel of the holiness of God and the costliness of sin. But as the writer of Hebrews says, "It is impossible for the blood of bulls and goats to take away sins." And he concludes that "it is by God's will that we have been sanctified through the offering of the body of Jesus Christ once for all" (Heb. 10:4,10). Jesus Christ, who never sinned, became sin and accepted the judgment of God for us: "But he was wounded for our transgressions, crushed for our iniquities; upon him was the punishment that made us whole, and by his bruises we are healed" (Isa. 53:5).

Considering the awesome price Jesus paid for us, the cross also speaks to us of God's love and mercy. On my office wall hangs a painting titled "The Prodigal." That painting means a lot to me because, like the Prodigal, I spent years rebelling against my Lord. If you had known me, you might not have realized it, though. On the outside, I looked good; inside, my attitudes were another story. But the loving rebuke of my older brother brought me to my senses, so that I could repent and return to the Father. I was keenly aware of what was wrong in my life and knew I deserved to be punished. But God took me by surprise. Instead of punishing me, he forgave me—based on Jesus' death on the cross. His mercy melted my heart.

Jesus. Sin. Mercy. Three important words in the message of the cross. Some survey the cross and walk away, calling its message "foolishness." Others have eyes to see a Love so amazing and divine that it demands their all. No one can ignore the power of the cross of Jesus Christ.

What part of the message of the cross do you most need to hear today? What message is sounding in your heart in this quiet moment?

Father, give me ears to hear what your cross says to me and a willing heart to embrace all that the cross requires of me today.

1. Sin is not wrong doing — but wrong being.

2. Heb 10:4,10 "it is by God's will that we have been sanctified through the offering of the body of Jesus Christ once for all."

REVIVAL THROUGH CONFESSION

If we say that we have no sin, we deceive ourselves, and the truth is not in us. If we confess our sins, he who is faithful and just will forgive us our sins and cleanse us from all unrighteousness.

1 John 1:8–9

The cross of Christ stands powerfully before us, providing all we need to live deeply satisfying, godly lives. But that power can be obscured by sin in our lives that builds through our neglect and insensitivity to God's commands. At that point, personal revival becomes crucial, if we are ever to know again that power in our lives.

I enjoy reading of the faithful people God uses to bring about spiritual renewal. Their stories encourage me. For example, in Wales, early in the 1900s, Evan Roberts preached a message of simple truth, of four steps to spiritual renewal, and people prayerfully heard and began to seek the Lord. The revival in their lives changed the spiritual course of that country—and its impact was felt around the world.

Those four steps to spiritual renewal seem as relevant today as they were when Roberts preached them nearly a century ago. In fact, God used them to turn my life around.

Roberts first admonished the Welsh people to acknowledge to God any sin they were aware of. The Bible says, "No one who conceals transgressions will prosper, but one who confesses and forsakes them will obtain mercy" (Prov. 28:13). *Confessing sin,* the first step, may sound relatively simple, but one of sin's characteristics is deception. It can be difficult to see sin for what it is, to call it what God calls it. We may think someone else's sin intolerable, while the same sin in our life seems reasonable.

To illustrate, I'll tell you of an event when my desire to minister became my spiritual Achilles' heel. I came to the auditorium where I was to sing that night expecting to have a full concert. But the sponsor had also invited an evangelist to speak. Neither of us knew that the other was coming. You can imagine our surprise. Nevertheless, we attempted to work out a shared program. I tried my best to fit into the program, but the evangelist ignored me until I felt invisible. At one point, he even knocked over my guitar as he walked across the stage.

As the evening drew to a close and the invitation was given, I was irritated and my heart was hard. And I felt justified in my anger. Hadn't I been treated badly? Later, in my time alone with God praying and reading Scripture, I saw what was really in my heart —*pride.* I was more concerned about being slighted than about the souls of those who had come to the meeting. I kneeled and asked God's forgiveness for my sin.

Without that time with the Lord, immersing myself in the Word, I doubt I would have so readily seen my sin. It is easy to be deceived. But when we look into the mirror of Scripture, God reveals what is in our hearts.

Confession begins with honesty before our Creator, and a sincere desire to make things right with him. When we do, we can echo the words of the psalmist: "Search me, O God, and know my heart; test me and know my thoughts. See if there is any wicked way in me, and lead me in the way everlasting" (Ps. 139:23–24).

Have you looked in the mirror of God's Word lately? Is confession —the first step to spiritual renewal—continually a part of your life?

Father, I know that nothing is hidden from your sight and if I conceal my sin I will not prosper. So, prompted by your Spirit I humbly confess my sin to you and receive your forgiveness.

Hiding
Running
Judging others
Not wanting to go to work
Laziness
No discipline
No trust in you - God
Completing what I start
Jealousy
Comparing myself
Not a person of my word
Complacent
Spending money
 - Wanting "things"
Greed
 - Wanting everything
   - in the world
   - & you too God
   - my heart is still divided

3

REVIVAL THROUGH RESTITUTION

*Leave your gift there before the
altar and go; first be reconciled
to your brother or sister . . .*

Matthew 5:24

The word *revival* sometimes conjures up
images of religious hoopla. When God renews
us it *is* exciting, but the process can be soul-
wrenching. *Revival* really means being
rescued from the clutches of evil and sin, and
returning in loving obedience to our Lord.
And confession is the start of revival.

Evan Roberts, the Welsh revivalist, pointed
out that *restitution* is another necessary
element of revival. Restitution—making right
any wrong we've done to another person—is
the second step to spiritual renewal.

Zaccheus knew about restitution. When he
met Jesus, he said, "Look, half of my
possessions, Lord, I will give to the poor; and
if I have defrauded anyone of anything, I will
pay back four times as much" (Luke 19:8).
This tax collector, longing for a clear

conscience, admitted his dishonesty and wanted to make right the wrongs he had done to others. A clear conscience comes after I have gone to everyone I have wronged, sinned against, stolen from or hurt, and attempted to make the situation right.

Satan wants us to think our sin is too small to make right, but big enough that we never forget it. By keeping the memory of our sin pressing on our minds, he spiritually blackmails us to keep us powerless.

One night after I gave a concert, a man came to talk to me. He trembled as he told me that he needed to be set free. He didn't tell me details, and I didn't need to know. He explained that something had kept him bound and that he even feared for his life. When I asked him if he'd told his pastor, he said, "No, I could never tell him." Then I asked if he had told his wife, reminding him that sin or disobedience affects those around us. He responded, "I'd rather die than tell my wife."

Then I told him the hard truth, "That is exactly what you'll have to do—humble yourself, and die to your pride." I encouraged him not to underestimate the grace and forgiveness the Lord pours out on us, and the restoration God brings to our relationships.

This is not a trivial matter. Do not rest until you have settled the issue of a clear conscience. We can never go on with the Lord until we return to the point of our sin and deal with it in God's way. Only then can we experience genuine spiritual revival.

Today, has God reminded you of a broken relationship with someone? Is there something you need to do to clear your conscience?

Holy Lord, how can I expect to be filled with your Spirit if my conscience is polluted? No matter how small the matter, I will humble myself and make right the wrong I have done. Thank you for the strength to do this.

I don't even think I'm close to being able to have my family as part of my present.

I use to think we were so close. Couldn't go a week without calling. I really need your help w/ this God. My Parents are older & both are facing crippling/terminal diseases & I totally shut down towards them.

Please help us all!

I lay down this area to you God— I choose to give this shut down/block to you God. I don't want my parents to die & I don't even care!

4

Revival Through Obedience

If by the Spirit you put to death the deeds of the body, you will live. For all who are led by the Spirit of God are children of God.

Romans 8:13–14

We already have looked at the importance of confession and restitution to spiritual revival. Evan Roberts's message also emphasized the principle of *obedience*, encouraging us to "put away any doubtful habit" and "obey the Spirit promptly."

Are there things you do that are "doubtful"? Ask yourself these questions about any suspect activity or behavior:

- *Is this fitting of me as a Christian?*
- *Can I do this and not sin—or is this contrary to the Word of God?*
- *Will this set me up for a fall, or will it cause someone else to fall?*

If any of these questions raise doubts about the habit, consider giving it up. Since the Spirit of God lives in us, we cannot rationalize sin.

Paul says, "Put on the Lord Jesus Christ, and make no provision for the flesh, to gratify its desires" (Rom. 13:14). *No provision.* The Lord constantly reminds me of that. No part of our being—not our eyes, mind, thoughts, heart, hands or feet should have anything to do with evil. Paul also writes, "I appeal to you therefore, brothers and sisters, by the mercies of God, to present your bodies as a living sacrifice, holy and acceptable to God, which is your spiritual worship" (Rom. 12:1).

The other side of this coin is learning to obey the Spirit promptly. Sometimes I call my children and they respond, "Coming, Dad." Several minutes pass, and still no children in sight . . . Their response was immediate, but there was no follow-through. Obedience is not what we *say*, but what we *do*.

This spiritual principle is tough to put into practice. I remember a disagreement I had with my wife, Marijean, on the day of a concert. I knew that my words had hurt her. But I left to help at the auditorium, and did not see her until our group prayer time, right before the concert. We all prayed, but still I did not apologize to her. Later in the evening, she joined me on the platform to sing a duet, "I Cherish the Treasure of You." I was terribly uncomfortable. How could I sing that with her? I knew that if I pretended nothing was wrong, I would not only wound her further, but also grieve the Holy Spirit. What was I to do? Stop the concert and apologize right there?

That's exactly what I had to do if I was to obey the Spirit. So I asked the audience to give me a moment with Marijean, and right there on stage I asked her forgiveness for being harsh with her. My heaviness lifted, and the rest of the evening I felt joy and freedom in the Lord.

Revival and obedience go hand in hand. The writer to the Hebrews reminds us, "Today, if you hear his voice, do not harden your hearts" (Heb. 3:7–8).

Are any of your habits doubtful? Have you checked them with the three questions on page 11? Can you think of times when your faith has been revived through prompt obedience to the Holy Spirit?

Dear Lord, though I say that I love you, the evidence of my love is obedience to your Word. Please give me grace today to obey you.

5

REVIVAL THROUGH TESTIMONY

Tell of his salvation from day to day. Declare his glory among the nations, his marvelous works among all the peoples.

Psalm 96:2–3

What are we called to do in our world? As Welsh evangelist Evan Roberts indicated in his sermon long ago, we are to tell others how the Lord has transformed our lives. That's it —we are called to be living witnesses of Christ's love and grace.

Every believer has a story. Through the years I have collected biographies of Christians whose lives are great examples of faith. Marijean and I recently read to our children the story of John Newton, who wrote the beloved hymn, "Amazing Grace." Newton once was a vile person, the owner of a slave ship. That's why, when he finally gave his heart to the Lord, he penned these words:

Amazing grace, how sweet the sound that saved a wretch like me.

Before I discovered the power of the cross to change my heart, I was no better than

Newton. Outwardly, my life did not look as bad as his, but inwardly, apart from the Lord, my heart was wretched. With my new heart, I soon had opportunity to let others know of God's greatness—simply by telling my story.

I remember boarding an early flight one morning from Atlanta to the West Coast. I had a good book to read and was looking forward to some quiet. Nevertheless, I had given my day to the Lord, telling him I was available for anything he had for me. Soon a young guy with a beer in his hand came down the aisle grumbling and looking for his seat. I thought to myself, *Whoever he sits by is in for a treat!* You guessed it. His seat was next to mine.

After we introduced ourselves, Kip told me he was angry about his seat assignment. He had requested a seat in the smoking section (this was before the ban on smoking on planes), but he arrived at the ticket counter to discover his reservation had been lost. The only seat left was next to me in non-smoking.

As we talked, I sensed that his pain was deeper than that. Before the plane left the runway, he poured out the ache in his heart, telling me of the devastation in his life. That morning, before he left for the airport, he had prayed, "God, if you are real, help me find you." So he listened intently as I told him of the God I knew personally. A few hours later, somewhere between Atlanta and San Francisco, Kip prayed and came to know for himself Christ's power to change lives.

Not every opportunity to tell our stories will be as dramatic as that. But all the Lord wants is that we obey him and tell others what he has done for us. Telling our stories helps us remember where we were without Jesus Christ, and encourages us to keep living by faith.

Confession. Restitution. Obedience. Testimony. As Evan Roberts indicated nearly a century ago, these are pathways to spiritual revival.

What is your faith story? Are you ready to share the reason for your hope?

Gracious Lord, thank you for the privilege of telling others of your power to change lives. How can I be silent? May my life, today, point others to you, the source of life.

6
FAITHFULNESS

Let us hold fast to the confession of our hope without wavering, for he who has promised is faithful. And let us consider how to provoke one another to love and good deeds . . .

Hebrews 10:23–24

My parents, Charles and Jo Green, are missionaries. It's not unusual for people to say to them, "You've served the Lord so faithfully!" But they are quick to point out that faithfulness comes naturally in response to God's grace.

Faithfulness does not mean tightening our spiritual belts another notch and vowing that we're *really* going to do it this time. We have help. As the apostle Paul reminds the Philippian church, "It is God who is at work in you, enabling you both to will and to work for his good pleasure" (Phil. 2:13).

Nevertheless, Paul indicates that we have some responsibility when confronted with God's grace: "Therefore, my beloved, just as you have always obeyed me, not only in my presence, but much more now in my absence, work out your salvation with fear and trembling . . . " (Phil. 2:12). So we don't just sit day after day, saying, "Lord, make me faithful." God calls us to holy activity, to discipleship. We're here to transact God's business in our world. Our steps of faith and acts of love express our gratitude and trust in God who works in us.

We are well aware of our human frailties, but we take heart in biblical promises like this one: "His divine power has given us everything needed for life and godliness, through the knowledge of him who called us by his own glory and goodness" (2 Pet. 1:3). And we find hope in words like these, written to the Christians at Corinth: "And all of us, with unveiled faces, seeing the glory of the Lord as though reflected in a mirror, are being transformed into the same image from one degree of glory to another; for this comes from the Lord, the Spirit" (2 Cor. 3:18).

Listen to Jon Mohr's challenging, prayerful words in the song, "Find Us Faithful":

Oh, may all who come behind us
find us faithful.
May the fire of our devotion light their way.

But the song also makes clear that faithfulness in the lives of God's children is "a stirring testament to God's sustaining grace."

There is no room for one ounce of boasting, is there? Rather, it is God who takes our unfaithful lives and transforms them into lives that are steadfast. Faithfulness is what God wants, what he calls us to. And he provides the power we need to be faithful. We are saved by grace, we are kept by grace, all to his glory!

How is your spiritual equilibrium these days? Are you finding a balance in trusting the faithfulness of God and actively, obediently, responding to it?

Thank you for your divine power that has given me everything I need for life and godliness. Thank you too for your patience and the promise that you will complete the work that you started in me.

7

KNOWING AND BEING KNOWN

I know the one in whom I have put
my trust, and I am sure that he is
able to guard until that day
what I have entrusted to him.

2 Timothy 1:12

According to Gallop Polls, a large percentage of Americans claim to be Christians. But it can be difficult to find evidence that their lives have been significantly changed. Perhaps that's because we tend to think that coming to Christ means merely acknowledging his existence, learning some prayers and modifying a few behaviors.

In Christ's prayer for his disciples, he said, "And this is eternal life, that they may know you, the only true God, and Jesus Christ whom you have sent" (John 17:3). God has gone to great lengths to make himself known to us. And he is revealed most perfectly in Jesus Christ. As Scripture testifies, "No one has ever seen God. It is God the only Son, who is close to the Father's heart, who has made him known" (John 1:18).

How do we come to know him? By believing. Believing in Jesus encompasses all of life. Biblically, it means to be persuaded of, to rely upon, to obey, to trust in him. When Paul wrote to the Roman Christians, he described an intimate family relationship with God through Christ: "You have received a spirit of adoption. When we cry, 'Abba! Father!' it is that very Spirit bearing witness with our spirit that we are children of God" (Rom. 8:15–16).

Equally as wonderful as knowing the God of the universe, however, is that he knows me! One evening, I met some people who asked if I knew a friend of theirs. The friend, Tom, had told them he and I were good friends. I asked some questions to try to jog my memory, but I couldn't place him. It was embarrassing for us all. The truth was that although Tom and I apparently had met, he was not someone I knew.

Likewise, in Matthew 7, Jesus said that at the judgment many will call him "Lord, Lord," claiming to know him and telling of all the things that they had done in his name. But he will tell them plainly, "I never knew you." Not everyone who calls Jesus "Lord" will enter heaven, only those who do God's will.

Jesus said, "I am the good shepherd. I know my own and my own know me" (John 10:14). Do you have the comfort and assurance of knowing and being known by the Lord?

Lord Jesus, I do believe in you. With all my heart I long to know you and to be known as your very own.

8

HOME WHERE
WE BELONG

*I press on toward the goal for
the prize of the heavenly
call of God in Christ Jesus.*

Philippians 3:14

Scripture continually urges us to run,
endure, persevere and overcome. With that
imagery, we are apt to visualize a finish line at
the end of our pilgrimage. But we can't
imagine the glory of what lies beyond the goal.
And we are reminded that every effort,
sacrifice and suffering will be worth it when
we reach the goal and claim our prize. As the
apostle Paul wrote, "For this slight momentary
affliction is preparing us for an eternal weight
of glory beyond all measure" (2 Cor. 4:17).

So what is our prize? What would fulfill our
deepest longings? Is it a crown or an award?
Maybe a position of cosmic importance?

It's even better than that. Ever since sin
entered the human race with Adam and Eve,
we have been *homeless.* I believe what we all

yearn for is *home*. A home where we, at last, belong.

When I was four years old, my family moved from Arizona to South America to serve as missionaries. In northern Argentina where we lived, I grew to love the people, but I always felt like a foreigner. Our furloughs back in the States only intensified my desire to move home to Arizona. Finally, after high school, I returned to Phoenix to enroll in college. I thought that surely would satisfy my longing for home. Yet, I discovered I had been out of the United States so long that I didn't quite fit in—Arizona wasn't really *home* either.

It wasn't until years later that I discovered what I really longed for—my heavenly home. And I'm not alone in my longing. Through the years the people of God have recognized that they are "aliens and strangers on earth," looking for a better country—a heavenly one.

Jesus knew how to comfort his disciples in their greatest need. He told them he was going to prepare a place for them, and that one day he would come back and take them to be with him: "Do not let your hearts be troubled . . . In my Father's house there are many dwelling places . . . And you know the way to the place where I am going" (John 14:1–4).

Everything around us—from the decay of the environment to the depths of human corruption—reminds us that this world is not our real home. The faint strains of eternity echo in our hearts, creating a gnawing ache for the presence of our Lord. We try to settle the uneasiness in our souls with what the world offers, but nothing satisfies.

Augustine declared, "Thou madest us for thyself, and our heart is restless, until it repose in thee." *Home* is where Jesus is. It is where we are free at last from every fleshly desire and crippling weakness caused by the curse of sin. It is the only place that cures the restlessness in our hearts, where we will never again chase after emptiness. *Home* is where all tears are dried and every wrong is made right. There can be no better prize than, through Jesus, to find home. "For we know that if the earthly tent we live in is destroyed, we have a building from God, a house not made with hands, eternal in the heavens" (2 Cor. 5:1).

How do you describe the longing in your heart that never goes away, no matter how well things are going? Have you ever thought you might be homesick?

Dear Jesus, thank you for the hope and promise of heaven, where I will be with you forever. Thank you also for this longing in my heart. It keeps me looking forward to your return. Come quickly, Lord.

9

UNTIL WE GET THERE

*"And remember, I am with you
always, to the end of the age."*

Matthew 28:20

As Jesus prepared to return to the Father,
he told his disciples, "I am with you only a
little longer. You will look for me; and as I
said to the Jews so now I say to you, 'Where I
am going, you cannot come'" (John 13:33).

Imagine the disciples' sorrow and
bewilderment. The one they had left everything for was now leaving them. The one who
had cared for them, provided for their every
need, and loved them like they had never
been loved, was abandoning them. Did Jesus
understand how his words crushed them?
Then he answered the ache in their hearts, "I
will not leave you as orphans; I will come to
you."

Orphans! The word describes perfectly how
they felt. How like Jesus to know their hearts.
Although they did not understand it at the
time, he was speaking to them of the Holy
Spirit, whom the Father would send in his
name. The promise that Jesus gave to them
was that if they loved him and obeyed him,

then he and the Father would come and make their home not just *with* them but *in* them.

We are not orphans either. We have not been left alone. The promise of Jesus to his disciples is for us also. He said, "I will never leave you or forsake you." That is comforting.

Several years ago at a convention, I shared an afternoon concert with George Beverly Shea, the beloved soloist of the Billy Graham crusade team. We decided to sing a duet and he suggested an old Stuart Hamblen song.

This is what we sang:

But until then, my heart will go on singing,
Until then, with joy I'll carry on,
Until the day, my eyes behold the city,
Until the day, God calls me home.
(Stuart Hamblen, "Until Then")

Though we encounter difficulties in this life, we are not alone. Jesus is with us every step of the way, bringing joy to our journey.

Are you living today as if you were an orphan? Have you forgotten that Christ in you is the hope of glory, and all that he is, he is within you?

Thank you, Lord Jesus, for the reality of your presence. Awaken my senses, open my eyes, keep me aware of this glorious prize.

SAVORING THE WORD

O taste and see that the Lord is good;
happy are those who take refuge in him.

Psalm 34:8

God uses simple things to remind me of important spiritual principles. About three years ago, I had a virus that affected my tongue. Although the painful inflammation subsided in a couple of days, enlarged taste buds diminished my sense of taste for several more days.

One morning as I sat at the breakfast table finishing a "bitter" waffle, I thought of things that cause us to lose our taste for the Word of God. We all experience times when our emotions aren't in sync with our faith and the Lord seems far away. But spiritual weakness, resulting from giving in to the flesh, or a lack of peace, caused by rebellion or disobedience, can make the spiritual food of the Bible taste bitter to us.

David spoke of the Word as being "sweeter also than honey, and drippings of the honeycomb" (Ps. 19:10). At least that is how it should be to us. Are you delighting in the law of the Lord? What does Scripture taste like to you—a dry crust of bread or a satisfying meal?

Our taste buds also can be spoiled by eating too many sweets or other rich foods. Then, ordinary food becomes tasteless and boring. The only way to regain our taste for healthy food is to abstain from spicy treats and desserts until the staple foods become tasty again. Much the same way, maturing believers require a disciplined diet of solid spiritual food. We grow as we understand and apply by faith the deeper truths of God. The writer of Hebrews says, "But solid food is for the mature, for those whose faculties have been trained by practice to distinguish good from evil" (Heb. 5:14).

Does the meat of the Word taste good to you, or have your spiritual taste buds been spoiled by sensational teachings and distracting doctrines? There is no substitute for our own diligent study of the Scriptures. False teachers abound, but "we must no longer be children, tossed to and fro and blown about by every wind of doctrine . . . but speaking the truth in love, we must grow up in every way into him who is the head, into Christ" (Eph. 4:14–15).

If we want to be spiritually mature, firmly rooted in God's truth, we must savor and meditate on the Word of the Lord. Then we will be "like trees planted by streams of water, which yield their fruit in its season, and their leaves do not wither" (Ps. 1:3).

Has reading Scripture become a tasteless chore—or an anticipated blessing?

I praise you Lord for revealing yourself to me through the Scriptures. Forgive me for my complacency and for neglecting the privilege of knowing you through feasting on your Word.

Religion Or Relationship?

*Whom have I in heaven but you? And there
is nothing on earth that I desire other than
you. My flesh and my heart may fail, but
God is the strength of my heart and my
portion forever.*

Psalm 73:25–26

Pleasing others has always been important
to me. I remember presenting childhood
projects to my parents, anxious to receive their
praise. And the times I needed correction, a
look of disappointment from them was
enough to set me straight. As a young adult, I
always made an extra effort on the job to win
the favor of my employer. Nothing hurt me
more than knowing I had let someone down.

Not surprisingly, I am inclined to try to
please God by my own service. Not that there
is anything wrong with wanting to please God.
In fact, Paul told the Ephesians to "find out
what pleases the Lord." The danger is in
thinking that I can earn his favor by my works,
in concentrating more on what I can do for
God than on receiving what Christ has done

for me on the cross. And that is the difference
between mere religion and a vital relationship
with the Lord.

It is possible for any of us to be so caught
up in our own activity that we miss the
relationship the Lord wants us to have with
him. I've heard it said that Christians are
"saved to serve." So as soon as someone makes
a profession of faith, they are told to get busy
for the Lord.

But wait a minute. What is it that God is
after? Remember Enoch? We don't know
much about him except that he delighted so
much in God and brought such joy to him
that on one of their walks God simply took
him home. Or how about Abraham? He was
known as the "friend of God." I am
convinced, as Oswald Chambers said in *My
Utmost for His Highest,* that "God's main
concern is that we are more interested in him
than in work for him."

When asked to identify the greatest
commandment, Jesus replied, "Love the Lord
your God with all your heart and with all
your soul and with all your mind" (Matt.
22:37). Because of who God is and all he has
done for me, I can't help but love him. And I
express that love in worship and eager
obedience.

Is God the delight of your heart? Have you taken a break from your activity long enough to enjoy him?

Thank you, Lord, for restoring me to yourself through the power of the cross. Thank you for letting me know you and enjoy you today.

THE MIRACLE OF FORGIVENESS

Forgive, and you will be forgiven;
give, and it will be given to you . . .
for the measure you give will be
the measure you get back.

Luke 6:37–38

Flying is an adventure for me—I am fascinated with airplanes, and I enjoy meeting people. On one flight, I sat next to a retired university professor of biochemistry. After we got the introductions out of the way and our conversation deepened, he told me his story.

This man's sin against his wife and family had led to a divorce. From there, family relationships deteriorated to a smoldering hatred. The professor stayed away from church under the pretense that "scientists have no need for religion." All the while, the load of guilt he carried nearly crushed him.

Finally, in desperation, he began to search for God. He started attending church, where one Sunday morning he could stand his sin no longer and he cried out to the Lord for forgiveness. At that moment, the unbearable guilt began to ease and the chains around his heart loosened. In response to God's amazing forgiveness, this man humbly went to each family member he had wronged, to try to restore each relationship.

The professor's story reminded me of the miracle of forgiveness, and the crucial role it plays in the gospel. "In him we have redemption through his blood, the forgiveness of our trespasses, according to the riches of his grace" (Eph. 1:7). Holy God forgives us the only way possible—through the perfect sacrifice of Jesus Christ on the cross. The significance of God's gift of reconciliation compels us to turn—both to him and away from our sins. Our response to his grace is thankfulness and love.

How forgiving of others are we? Our answer will demonstrate how well we understand the extent of God's forgiveness of us. Remember Christ's parable of the ungrateful servant? He told of a king who mercifully canceled the large debt his servant was unable to pay. That same servant then turned around and had a friend thrown into prison for not paying a small debt he owed him. When the king heard of this, he confronted his servant: "Should you not have had mercy on your fellow slave, as I had mercy on you?" (Matt. 18:33).

Forgiving is a natural part of loving— tangible evidence of our life in Christ. Paul encouraged believers to "be kind to one another, tenderhearted, forgiving one another, as God in Christ has forgiven you" (Eph. 4:32). Although the wounds he suffered for our sins pierced his soul, Jesus responded, "Father, forgive them" (Luke 23:34). This same wondrous love "has been poured into our hearts through the Holy Spirit" (Rom. 5:5).

How can we forgive others for deep hurts, betrayals and injustices? At times it seems impossible. But by the power of his cross, the Lord gives us the ability to love even when we feel unloving, to be aware of our own weaknesses and to be merciful even in the midst of our pain.

Have you been deeply wounded by someone? If so, you may always bear the scars. But have you entrusted yourself to God's miracle of forgiveness?

Gracious Lord, my heart has been set free by your forgiveness. How can I ever thank you? By your power I will forgive those who have wronged me.

13

THE HEARTBEAT OF OUR MISSION

The water that I will give will become in them a spring of water gushing up to eternal life.

John 4:14

The old covenant called people to *do*—to obey God's commands. The new covenant compellingly invites us to *believe*, trusting in the finished work of Christ. Jesus said, "Out of the believer's heart shall flow rivers of living water" (John 7:38).

As long as achievements and position are our focus, we have forgotten our first priority —loving Christ, the source of all good things. If we depend on accomplishments for meaning in our lives, we are not making ourselves completely available to Christ, not willing to be broken bread and poured-out wine for the Master's purposes.

What if the Lord wants to take us out of the flow of activity for awhile, for renewal and teaching? What if we are to be hurt or to suffer for his glory? If our faith depends on outward accomplishment, then most likely we will be frustrated, restless, unwilling to submit to the refiner's fire. But if our relationship with the Lord is our source of well-being, his living water—his Spirit within our hearts—becomes the spring of our service. Ministry is a natural expression of Christ living in us.

When my son Josiah was about three, he entered the "I-can-do-it-by-myself" stage. Nothing I said could convince him that a task was too difficult for him. After many failed attempts, he finally would look at me with tender eyes and ask with a sigh, "Daddy, would you do this for me?"

Jesus said, "Apart from me you can do nothing" (John 15:5). When faced with overwhelming needs and countless challenges, don't run ahead of the Lord. Instead, run *to* him. Forsaking the springs of living water to dig our own cisterns of human resources leads to one thing—a dry well.

Certainly, our faith must be expressed in our actions: "For just as the body without the spirit is dead, so faith without works is also dead" (James 2:26). But carefully distinguish between service that is motivated by need, responsibility, guilt or attempts to gain the approval of God and others, and a life that becomes the fragrance of Christ, prompted and directed by the Lord who is supremely loved.

"The Mission," a song written by my friend Jon Mohr, beautifully summarizes this thought:

As the candle is consumed by the passion of the flame . . .
let us burn to know him deeper;
Then our service flaming bright will radiate his passions
and blaze with holy light.
To love the Lord our God is the heartbeat of our mission . . .

Is your love for God the heartbeat of your mission? Do your actions spring from the overflow of that relationship?

Heavenly Father, help me love you with my whole heart. Thank you for the power that works in me, providing the strength to serve you.

14

THE MARK OF LOVE

*So if I . . . have washed your feet, you also
ought to wash one another's feet.*

John 13:14

A story is told in John 12 of a dinner given
to honor Jesus. Martha served and her brother,
Lazarus, reclined at the table with Jesus. The
setting was familiar for that culture, but the
circumstances surrounding the evening were
nothing less than extraordinary. Not long
before, Jesus had raised Lazarus from the dead.
As a result, many Jews had put their faith in
Jesus. Having grown paranoid about Jesus'
growing popularity, the members of the
Jewish high court plotted to kill him.
Understandably, tension hung in the air that
night.

As the evening progressed, something
extraordinary briefly interrupted the dinner:
"Mary took a pound of costly perfume . . .
and anointed Jesus' feet, and wiped them
with her hair" (v. 3). The other guests were
indignant. "Why was this perfume not sold . .
. and the money given to the poor?" they

asked (v. 5). Jesus came to Mary's defense, calling her action spiritually significant.

Mary's outrageous act inspires us to worship. For true worship isn't a measured, sensible demonstration of loyalty and love—it is *extravagant.*

I once believed that love meant giving what I didn't need, hopefully to someone who received it with great appreciation. I thought love was giving something I wouldn't miss to one who believed I was making a sacrifice. But that's not love. True love "spends" far more than that.

The value of Mary's gift was obvious. Made of nard, a rare fragrant ointment, the perfume was worth a year's wages. But Mary didn't measure it out over a period of time or offer it with martyred sighs in hopes that Jesus would notice the value. She simply poured it out. Love costs us—but the expense means nothing to the one who truly loves.

If Jesus were here physically, I'd like to think I too would gladly spend some precious treasure on him. But I can love and anoint Jesus anyway. Scripture records his words, "Truly I tell you, just as you did it to one of the least of these who are members of my family, you did it to me" (Matt. 25:40). I love Jesus by loving his children. What I do in love to one of his own, he accepts as if it were done to himself.

And the house was filled with the fragrance of perfume. Sometimes our loving has no fragrance because it is masked by self-interest and vanity. Having grown stale through calculated and impersonal giving, our acts of love are a far cry from using our own hands and hair to wash a loved one's feet. The aroma of pure nard was distinctive, as is the fragrant outpouring of a disciple's heart in loving worship and service.

Do you see the face of Christ when you look into the eyes of a brother or sister in need? How extravagant is your love for the Lord you see there?

Lord Jesus, thank you for the privilege of demonstrating my love for you by loving others. Today, may my loving be extravagant.

15

FOR OUR GOOD

Discipline your children while there is hope; do not set your heart on their destruction.

Proverbs 19:18

An important part of parenting is disciplining our children. Discipline involves encouraging, teaching, guiding and nurturing —to develop in our kids strong spiritual character and a healthy relationship with God and others.

I remember one morning when my son, Josiah, who was five at the time, had been disobedient. I talked with him about his behavior and attitude, warning him that he would be disciplined if he persisted. But he disobeyed anyway and had to bear the consequences.

Afterwards, as I looked through tear-filled eyes at his tear-streaked face, I wondered if he could possibly understand the depth of my love for him. My greatest desire as his earthly father was that someday Josiah would wholeheartedly love and obey his heavenly Father.

A little later that day, Josiah was in my lap. I held him and assured him of my love, reminding him what a treasure he is to me. As he asked my forgiveness for his disobedience, his eyes reflected the tenderness of his little heart—and something eternal transpired. We went to breakfast together, just the two of us, and took a trip to the post office. All morning, he would not let me out of his sight. I remembered what God said: "Discipline your children, and they will give you rest; they will give delight to your heart" (Prov. 29:17).

Throughout that afternoon, I was reminded of these words: "'The Lord disciplines those whom he loves, and chastises every child whom he accepts.' Endure trials for the sake of discipline. God is treating you as children . . . he disciplines us for our good, in order that we may share his holiness" (Heb. 12:6–7,10).

What memories do you have of being disciplined as a child? Were you corrected in love, causing you to become more loving? Perhaps you were disciplined in anger. Or, you may have been traumatized by verbal abuse or have memories of being beaten. I am so sorry if this has been your experience. How this must break God's heart. That is not what he intended, nor how he treats his children.

The word *discipline* is just two letters away from *disciple*, implying a relational process of teaching. We experience this spiritual discipline when we are convicted by the Holy Spirit of any wrong attitude or action, directed by God's Word into the way of truth, or humbled through difficulties and suffering. No discipline seems pleasant at the time, but because God loves us, his discipline always is "for our good, in order that we may share in his holiness."

The psalmist said, "Happy are those whom you discipline, O Lord, and whom you teach out of your law" (Ps. 94:12). I often pray that God would draw my wandering heart back to himself, that he would not let me become hardened to his Word. If his discipline is evidence of his love, then I yearn for his correction.

How has the discipline you experienced as a child affected your concept of the Lord's correction? Do you trust your heavenly Father enough to welcome his loving discipline?

Thank you, Father, for your love that will not let me go. May my heart always be tender to your voice and responsive to your Word.

16

PROCEED WITH CAUTION

These things happened to them to serve as an example, and they were written down to instruct us, on whom the ends of the ages have come.

1 Corinthians 10:11

I once lived in a city crisscrossed by railroad tracks. When a train approached a crossing and the crossbars came down, people who had to wait sometimes grew impatient. They edged up to the bars, and if they thought they had a chance to beat the train, they drove around them. I always thought, *How foolish and dangerous to ignore the warning sign.* But that's human nature—and at times we all disregard the warnings.

Like the time I drove home from college through the mountains outside Flagstaff, Arizona. Roaring along in my '65 Mustang, I rounded the corner to see a police officer flashing his lights at me in warning. It unnerved me, and I slowed down. But fifteen minutes later, I was speeding again.

Often we don't take seriously the things we should. Unfortunately, warnings in Scripture can go unheeded too—like the sound of an alarm that we simply tune out. Remember Lot? He lived in the city of Sodom, a wicked and depraved place. Two angels arrived at the city in the evening and Lot invited them to his home for the night. The next few hours the men of the town surrounded Lot's house and treated the visitors to a terrifying display of unbridled lust and violence. The angels told Lot to get his family out of the city because they were going to destroy it. Lot pleaded with his sons-in-law to leave with him, but they thought he was joking. Listen to the narrative from Genesis: "When morning dawned, the angels urged Lot, saying, 'Get up, take your wife and your two daughters who are here, or else you will be consumed in the punishment of the city.' But he lingered; so the men seized him and his wife and his two daughters by the hand, the Lord being merciful to him, and they brought him out" (Gen. 19:15–16).

Time after time, Scripture alerts us to put on our armor, resist the devil, run from sexual immorality and abstain from sinful desires that would destroy our souls. How do we respond to these warnings? Biblical cautions are for our spiritual protection. They come from a loving, not vindictive, God who longs for us to experience the joy of a holy relationship.

The angels told Lot to run for his life, but he lingered. Are you carelessly ignoring any God-given warnings?

Lord, you are my Rock and my Salvation. When I remain in your protection I am safe. Thank you for every warning and caution in your Word. Today, may I be sensitive and alert to your voice.

17

BREAKING THE
HEART OF GOD

*"Jerusalem, Jerusalem, the city that kills
the prophets and stones those who are
sent to it! How often have I desired to
gather your children together as a hen
gathers her brood . . . and you
were not willing!"*

Matthew 23:37

The root of the human problem is *rebellion*, and we don't have to look far to find it. For example, I remember an incident when my daughter, Summer, was a little girl. We were playing a game together, and Summer kept taking game pieces that weren't hers. When I corrected her and told her, "Put that back," she burst into tears.

In disbelief I asked, "What on earth are you crying for?"

She sputtered, "It hurts my feelings when you tell me what to do."

"Honey, get used to it," I replied, "it happens to us all our lives!"

Nobody likes to be told what to do. That's the essence of sin, isn't it— rebellion against

God's authority. Scripture tells us that Israel "provoked him to anger" and that they "tested the Most High God, and rebelled against him. They did not observe his decrees, but turned away" (Ps. 78:56–57).

Rebellion comes in various forms. An example of *open rebellion* is found in the book of Jeremiah, after Jerusalem fell to Nebuchadnezzar and the Israelites were led into captivity. A remnant of Judeans escaped, but they disobeyed the Lord by going to Egypt and practicing idolatry. The prophet Jeremiah told them to expect disastrous consequences. But they answered, "We are not going to listen to you. Instead, we will do everything that we have vowed..." (Jer. 44:16–17).

When we openly rebel against God, we too reap terrible consequences. But God does not want us to go through the devastating pain that accompanies sin. Time and again, you hear the broken heart of the Lord in the words of the prophets: "I beg you not to do this abominable thing that I hate! . . . Why are you doing such great harm to yourselves . . . " (Jer. 44:4,7). And through Isaiah, God speaks as a grieving parent, "I reared children and brought them up, but they have rebelled against me . . . Why do you seek further beatings? Why do you continue to rebel? The whole head is sick and the whole heart faint" (Isa. 1:2, 5).

Remember that the God who, through Noah, called a world to repent waited more than one hundred years before he sent the flood waters.

And the crucified Savior looked down on his slayers with forgiveness.

The spiritual principles concerning open rebellion are as much about God's love and longing for us as they are about his power and authority over us. Rebellion breaks the heart of God.

Missionary-to-China Hudson Taylor said, "When the heart submits, Jesus reigns. And when Jesus reigns there is peace." Are you peace-full today?

Father, I bow before you, submitting to your authority. I offer every part of my life this day to you. You are my Lord and my God.

18

REFINED REBELLION

Return, O faithless children,
I will heal your faithlessness.
"Here we come to you;
for you are the Lord our God."

Jeremiah 3:22

We don't have to be openly defiant for
there to be a spark of rebellion smoldering
within us. *Refined rebellion,* more subtle than
open rebellion, is demonstrated in Christ's
parable of the two sons (Matt. 21:28–32).
When the father asked his sons to go work in
the vineyard, the first son said, "I will not."
But he later changed his mind and went. The
second son responded, "I will, sir," but he did
not go. The open rebellion of the first son
ended in repentance and obedience to the
father's will. But the second son did what I
call "saying a yes, but living a no."

Refined rebellion is poignantly described
in Jeremiah as God pleads with Israel to
repent: "For they have turned their backs to
me, and not their faces" (Jer. 2:27). Their
faces nodded a *yes* to the Lord, but their
hearts had already turned away.

Dr. James Dobson illustrates what I mean by refined rebellion with a story of a father who told his little boy to sit down in his chair. The boy complied, but muttered, "I may be sitting down on the outside, but I'm standing up on the inside!" That was me when I was growing up. Outwardly, I complied with the requirements of my family and home, but inwardly, I resented doing it. That's where rebellion grows, inside the heart. And slowly, gradually, my heart became hardened against the Lord.

The only answer for rebellion is repentance —a change of heart, a turning from sin to God. This was God's call to Israel. It was the call of Jesus and John the Baptist. Repentance comes when we see in the cross of Christ a symbol both of our depravity and rebellion *and* of God's love and mercy. We admit that sin has profaned our hearts, and that we are unable to save ourselves. "But this is the one to whom I will look, to the humble and contrite in spirit, who trembles at my word" (Isa. 66:2).

The Lord doesn't ask us to bring pure and perfect hearts to him. Instead, we place our penitent, pliable hearts in his hands. That is our hope. These beautiful words from Isaiah affirm God's promise of help and healing: "I dwell in the high and holy place, and also with those who are contrite and humble in spirit, to revive the spirit of the humble, and to revive the heart of the contrite . . . I have seen their ways, but I will heal them; I will lead them and repay them with comfort . . . " (Isa. 57:15,18).

We sometimes confuse sensitivity with spirituality. Yet it is possible to be both sensitive and rebellious. Is there any hardness in your heart towards God?

Father, in an age of independence and rebellious living, I submit my feelings, desires and thoughts to you. In all my ways, I want to acknowledge you, my Lord.

19

HEART OF HEARTS

With my whole heart I seek you; do not let me stray from your commandments.

Psalm 119:10

Several years ago, I gave a concert in the Midwest. Afterwards, because it was late, Marijean took the kids back to the hotel, and I went out with the concert sponsors to get something to eat and to unwind. By the time I got back to the hotel, Marijean already had put the kids to bed and was asleep.

I wasn't sleepy yet, so I thought about turning on the TV. That sounds harmless, doesn't it? I often have confessed to others that the unwholesome TV fare in hotels can be dangerous. I know the deceptiveness in my own heart. But no one would know . . . What would be the harm?

And then this thought popped into my mind: *Steve, who you are in secret is who you really are.*

The Lord has been reminding me that what happens in the secret places of my heart where no one else can see is who I really am.

It is easy to live for externals—to be

satisfied if people think well of us. And it is easy to ignore what is going on inside us, things no one else can see.

Jesus talked a lot about this. In his Sermon on the Mount, he exposed the hypocrisy of those who loved to pray on the street corner or disfigure their faces when fasting so that others would think them spiritual. He said, "Truly I tell you, they have received their reward." They had missed the heart of God, which declares, "Your Father who sees in secret will reward you" (Matt. 6:5–6).

For many years, I too was a "performer." If someone saw my Bible open and assumed I had been reading it, I was happy—whether I had read it or not. Because we all want people to like us, we can fool them by acting religious, even if we've never had a true encounter with God. But the Bible says, "Before him no creature is hidden, but all are naked and laid bare to the eyes of the one to whom we must render an account" (Heb. 4:13).

I still am a recovering hypocrite. Daily, I pray for the humility to live transparently, not pretending to be one step further along than I really am.

How about you? What are you like when

no one is looking? God, in his love, has made us new creations in Christ. By the power of the cross, he has freed us from our sins and brought us into his light. As children of light, let's reject all deception and welcome truth in our inmost being.

Is there an area of your life that you are ashamed of? Will you come to the One who loves you most and be honest with him? Will you take full advantage of his provision in Christ to live free from sin?

Lord, you know everything about me. You know every flaw and weakness, every hidden thing. Please save me from hypocrisy. Today, I want to live every moment in the light of your presence.

20

HINDRANCES TO HOLINESS

*Since we have these promises,
beloved, let us cleanse ourselves from
every defilement of body and of spirit,
making holiness perfect in the fear of God.*

2 Corinthians 7:1

After my concerts, people often stay to talk with me. Sometimes they ask for prayer. One woman told me she and her husband were separated and asked me to pray for her. "I'm sorry," I said. "What happened?"

She replied, "He's really the nicest man I know, a great husband. But I left him because I'm restless and I don't know if I can stay married. Pray that I'll know what to do."

My reaction was this: *Why pray when God already has clearly revealed his will?*

Just as we tend to view posted speed limits as merely suggestions, sometimes we view biblical commands the same way. But God's *commands* are just that—commands. Instead of a burden, though, they are the path to freedom.

When God asks us to do something, he gives us everything we need to do it. Our responsibility is to obey him and to take advantage of his provision.

Scripture indicates that our power comes through Christ's death on the cross. "We know that our old self was crucified with him so that the body of sin might be destroyed, and we might no longer be enslaved to sin . . . So you also must consider yourselves dead to sin and alive to God in Christ Jesus" (Rom. 6:6,11).

A few years ago, I took some time off, went to a cabin and read Jerry Bridges's book, *The Pursuit of Holiness*. As I read, I asked God to show me where my life didn't conform to his Word. This is what I learned:

I saw that one thing that hinders my holiness is my tendency to categorize sin. Labeling sins according to how serious they are can become a way to excuse my behavior. I rationalized, *I'm a good person, and I don't do any of the horrible sins. Surely this little sin won't matter to God.* But who am I to say what sin is little and what is big? If God is holy, every one of his commands is to be obeyed. My sins grieve him, despite my attempt to call them other names and to rationalize their significance.

Another pitfall for me is subscribing to

"cultural holiness"—conforming my responses to God's commands to what I see others around me doing. For example, if all the church people do something I may otherwise consider questionable, I think it must be okay for me too.

But that's not so. Once, my kids asked if we could rent a video that some of their church friends had seen. I asked them if there was anything in the video they thought would hurt God. They replied, "Um, just two little places—but really most of it is very good and funny." God provides much for us to enjoy in this world, but even in the "little things" we must base our actions on the Lord's Word and his character. This is our holy "response-ability."

"All deeds are right in the sight of the doer, but the Lord weighs the heart" (Prov. 21:2). Are you trusting your own feelings and thoughts, or are you submitting all your ways to the Lord?

Holy Father, holiness is who you are and what you require of us. Thank you that Christ Jesus has made us holy in your sight. Praise you that with Christ in us we are being conformed to your likeness.

21

Born Of God

*But to all who received him, who believed
in his name, he gave power to become
children of God, who were born, not of
blood or of the will of the flesh or of the will
of man, but of God.*

John 1:12–13

What does it mean to be born of God? A
number of years ago, I came across a tract by
J. C. Ryle that pointed out the evidences of
new birth in Christ, as listed in 1 John. There
we find several standards of faith. The Bible
exhorts us to examine ourselves in light of
these standards to be sure we are in the faith.

The first evidence of faith, *turning from
sin,* is found in 1 John 3:9: "Those who have
been born of God do not sin, because God's
seed abides in them; they cannot sin, because
they have been born of God." It may be true,
as the bumper sticker says, that "Christians
aren't perfect; they're just forgiven." But that
doesn't excuse our sin. If we have been born
again, we are new creations in Christ. Once
we were sinners by nature, disobedient to
God. Now we struggle against sin; we run

from it and grieve any time we fall under its influence. Sin no longer pleases us. As God's children, we do not sin as a way of life, but live for the Lord.

The second evidence of faith is *knowing Jesus*: "Everyone who believes that Jesus is the Christ has been born of God" (1 John 5:1). Believers know that there is no one besides Jesus who can save us. At times we may not feel much like children of God and may be discouraged by our slow spiritual growth. But on what do we base our salvation? Certainly not on our goodness or our spiritual activities. We do not look to our family heritage, church membership or pastor for spiritual security. Rather, we affirm with the great hymn,

> *My hope is built on nothing less than*
> *Jesus' blood and righteousness.*
> *I dare not trust the sweetest frame, but*
> *wholly lean on Jesus' name.*

("Christ the Solid Rock," words by Edward Mote and Elma Hendrix)

The third evidence of our faith is *doing what is right:* "Everyone who does right has been born of him" (1 John 2:29). Christians can readily admit weaknesses and failures. And though waves of temptation may batter us, our course is set. Our lives are turned toward the Lord. And all our actions indicate that Christ lives in us, and that our heart's desire is to do what is right.

How well do you measure up to the three standards of faith listed above? Even if you have never accepted the good news of the gospel, there is still time. Humble yourself, confess your sin and trust in Jesus Christ as the one who saves you.

Lord and Savior, thank you for the gift of salvation. Thank you for the promise that everyone who calls on you will be saved.

22

BORN TO LOVE, BORN TO OVERCOME

Now that you have purified your souls by your obedience to the truth so that you have genuine mutual love, love one another deeply from the heart. You have been born anew, not of perishable but of imperishable seed, through the living and enduring word of God.

1 Peter 1:22–23

Those born of God are in synch with God's nature and will. In John's first letter to the churches, we see more clearly the practical meaning of this spiritual birth. John says, "We know that we have passed from death to life because we love one another" (1 John 3:14). Although Christians are compassionate to all people, we have a unique bond with other believers. Differences in race, economic standing or cultural background do not matter because we are family—God's family.

I love to visit my friends at New York City's Brooklyn Tabernacle. The last time I was there, pastor Jim Cymbala asked the people in the congregation to identify their native countries. There must have been twenty different nationalities represented. But all differences dissolved in light of our common bond in Jesus. As part of the body of Christ we are joined together by his Spirit. We are fellow pilgrims, submitting to the same Lord and warring against the same enemy, Satan. For all these reasons, we are never so happy as when we are with other believers.

In the last chapter of 1 John we read, "For whatever is born of God conquers the world. And this is the victory that conquers the world, our faith" (1 John 5:4). We believers know that sinful cravings, the lust of the eyes and boasting about possessions and position don't come from the Father but from the world. We realize that the world and its desires are only temporary, but those who do the will of God live forever. We know that getting too cozy with the world alienates us from God. Consequently, the world's pleasures, passions, profits, values and rewards are not our desire. Rather, we aim to please God by trusting and obeying him.

God's power frees us to live in a completely new way. We aren't simply pretending to be changed, for if we were, our true nature eventually would be revealed. Although we may fail at times, we still are new creations in Christ. This miracle comes about when the Holy Spirit moves into our lives, giving us life instead of death.

Has the Spirit of God confirmed in your spirit that you belong to him? Do you sense a unique bond with other believers?

Dear Lord, thank you for choosing me before you even created the world. Thank you for giving me life in Christ, even when I was dead in sin. I praise you, because every part of my salvation is by your doing.

23

PRAYING IN EARNEST

O you who answer prayer! To you all flesh shall come. When deeds of iniquity overwhelm us, you forgive our transgressions.

Psalm 65:2–3

On August 14, 1983, prayer became a vital part of my life.

Before that day, I prayed before meals, or if I had a crisis, or had to make an important decision. But my prayers didn't reflect a deep love for the Lord and a desire to stay close to him.

You'd never know it by looking at my credentials. I was reared in a Christian family with missionary parents. I was a backup singer for a popular Christian musical group, and my own singing career was growing. But more and more, I became a servant of sin, mostly in my thoughts and desires.

On that August afternoon in 1983, the Lord used my older brother, Randy, to lovingly confront me. We were riding with other family members to visit a relative who was in the hospital. Randy, who had recently experienced a personal revival, had been exhorting us for three days. This day was no different. As we drove, he began talking about personal holiness. I interrupted him with wisecracks, and kept changing the subject. When he continued, I became angry and told him to be quiet. In the uneasy silence that followed, Randy began to cry. He turned to me and said, "Steve, you're not resisting me. You are resisting the Holy Spirit. God wants to use you, but there is something wrong in your heart. I beg you to get right with God."

I felt exposed—humiliated in front of my family—and a host of emotions surged through me, including confusion, defensiveness and self-righteous anger. But along with all those feelings came the gnawing thought that Randy was right. By the end of the day I was in turmoil as I realized how hypocritical I had become.

That evening, in desperation, I kneeled and confessed my sins, saying, "Lord, have mercy on me. I have said 'no' to you for so long. Tonight, I say 'yes' to all your will." No bells went off, no lightning bolts struck. But the next day, I awoke knowing God was changing my desires.

After I boarded a plane to fly to Atlanta to sing, I began writing down my thoughts: *My*

*desire is to know God, the power of his
resurrection and the fellowship of his suffering.
How can I find him? . . . I want the power of
God manifest in my life, to show that he is a
consuming fire, able to save, purify and make
us righteous in the midst of a diseased world.*

In my hotel room that night, I didn't flip
on the TV as usual. Instead, I got on my knees
and prayed longer than I ever had before. The
following day I continued writing my
thoughts: *Is the cost of consecration and
surrender too high? Not if I'm sick of carnality
and tepid spiritual life, not if I'm sick of a
bland relationship with no burning love and
no power.* Then I asked God to revive my first
love at any cost.

Now as I reread those journal entries, I'm
grateful to God for speaking through my
brother Randy. I wonder what turn my life
would have taken if I had said *no* to the Holy
Spirit.

**Have you taken time today to pray in
earnest?**

*Lord, you see every part of our lives. Nothing
is hidden from you. Thank you for the promise
that if we humble ourselves and pray and seek
your face and turn from our sin, you will hear
and forgive.*

24

LETTERS TO GOD

Devote yourselves to prayer, keeping alert in it with thanksgiving.

Colossians 4:2

For several years now I have written my prayers in a journal—as though I'm writing a letter to God. Some days I'll begin with "Dear Father," other days "Gracious God," sometimes simply "Abba." Then I talk to him, writing out my praises, confessions and requests.

Prayer is a difficult discipline, especially since our lives move so fast. If I don't fight for time with the Lord, it won't happen. And I desperately need that contact with God to stay spiritually sensitive. I've found that writing prayer letters keeps my thoughts focused and allows me time to think about my conversation with God.

Sometimes my journal entries don't make much sense; sometimes they're tear-stained. It's personal stuff, expression of my heart's cries to the Lord. That's what he wants to hear. What matters isn't how good it looks on paper, but how responsive I am to his will.

Through the pressures of daily life I can become hardened, almost imperceptibly, until I have lost my tenderness and Christlikeness. It is during prayer that sensitivity is restored —when temporary things look temporary and eternal things eternal.

Even my wife, Marijean, can detect the change in my heart after a time of prayer. More than once she has said with a smile, "I like it when you spend time with the Lord." She has a gentle way of rebuking me!

In a way, prayer is like my relationship with Marijean. During our courtship, a whole lot of feeling and emotion was evident. Fifteen years later some of that remains, but more importantly, our love and understanding have deepened.

Since the heart-wrenching turnaround in my life in 1983, I've come to know the Lord more intimately. I'm now convinced of who he is, of his reality. My faith has grown and my prayers more closely echo his heart. Prayer now is a way of life for me, reflecting my longing to stay close to God.

Every once in a while I'll see a dramatic answer to my prayers. But more often than not it's just a steady, non-flashy, day-to-day communion with God—and the deep reward of living intimately with my Creator.

Is prayer a way of life for you? Have you ever written a letter to God?

Dear Father, forgive me for my lack of faith and prayerlessness. I want to know you. Please grace your child to seek you diligently.

25

"Daddy, My Hand Hurts"

I run the way of your commandments, for you enlarge my understanding.

Psalm 119:32

Years ago, I was on tour in Canada and was asked to sing on a morning television program. During the airing of the show, Marijean and our four-year-old, Summer, sat behind the main set watching a monitor so they could see Daddy sing. When her attention waned, Summer explored the studio. There she found a jar of glass beads and asked if she might take them with her back to the hotel. We said no, explaining that they belonged to the people at the TV station.

An hour later we had finished the program, browsed through a bookstore and finally were on our way back to the hotel. Just as the driver started down the street, Summer said, "Daddy, my hand hurts." I looked down and saw her clenched fist, but could not see what she held. I asked her to show me—and she opened her fingers, revealing a handful of the glass beads. She had been holding them tightly, and quietly, for a half hour.

After talking with Summer about stealing, I asked the driver to take us back to the station. I accompanied her inside as she returned the beads and asked for forgiveness.

On our way home I thought of her remark, "My hand hurts." We too experience discomfort when we hold on to something not meant for us. How many times have I cried out to God in anguish, only to have him reveal to me some disobedience in my desire.

Holding on to a grudge while harboring unforgiveness against someone only poisons our hearts. Grasping for some material possession and clinging to it draws us into idolatry. Refusing to let go of some secret sin only gives the Enemy of our souls an opportunity to attack us.

What are you holding onto that is causing you pain? Are you willing to let it go?

Loving Father, I acknowledge that your will for me is good, perfect and pleasing. There is great joy in embracing all your ways.

26

JUDGEMENT

*For we must all appear before
the judgment seat of Christ, that
each one may receive what is due
him for the things done while in the
body, whether good or bad.*

2 Corinthians 5:10 (NIV)

I recently made an unexpected trip to the
dentist. My daughter, Summer, could not
keep her regular cleaning and checkup
appointment, so I took her place. I really don't
mind getting my teeth cleaned; it's just that I
didn't have time to prepare. You see, the week
before my checkup I spend a little extra time
on my teeth.

I have the world's most thorough dental
hygienist. Nothing escapes her observation.
As she worked on me, I noticed that my gums
were more sensitive than normal. Any minute
I feared she would ask the dreaded question. I
thought of excuses: *I had been in the recording
studio until late at night and was simply too
tired. I had forgotten. So what if I had missed
a few nights. What's so bad about that?*

Vicki interrupted my thoughts. "Have you
been flossing regularly?" she asked.

I had to tell the truth. "No," I replied.

As I sat under the spotlight, with Vicki inspecting every tooth, I thought of a Bible verse: "Nothing in all creation is hidden from God's sight. Everything is uncovered and laid bare before the eyes of him to whom we must give account" (Heb. 4:13, NIV). Here I was, sitting in the judgment seat of Vicki, realizing that some day I will give an account to him whose eyes are like fire and who knows every thought and motive. What will it be like? How can I endure such scrutiny? Here's what I've been thinking about that day of judgment.

First, the Judge is our friend. That's encouraging. He saved us, laying down his own life to buy us back from sin. He gave us his word, explaining all that he wants us to know. He gives us warnings, instructions and encouragement to keep us on track. More than all this, he lives in us by the Holy Spirit, so that we can do all that he requires. What a friend! He is with us every step of the way, able to keep us from falling, till the day we stand before him.

Next, because our appearing before Christ is in the future, there is the temptation to grow lax. Because our sin often does not bring immediate consequences, it is possible to carry on almost as if nothing has happened.

When I was a boy in Argentina, I traveled with my father to a nearby town for a Bible conference. Once there, my father warned me not to go into a neighboring village because they were celebrating "carnival." Their festivals were vile and possibly dangerous for me. But curiosity won the battle for my will and I climbed the hill to see what what was going on. As I came back down to the conference, someone saw me and told my dad. He let me know that when we got home that afternoon he would have to discipline me. That gave me about three hours to sweat and suffer with knots in my stomach.

My dad preached a message and talked with the people. I even saw him laughing. When we got in the car to go home, he spoke to me kindly. *He's forgotten,* I said to myself. *Could it be possible? Maybe he has softened a bit and will just give me a warning.*

As we pulled into our driveway, he turned and said, "Steve, I want to see you in my room." He hadn't forgotten—and I wouldn't either!

Although the Judge is my friend, he does not show favoritism. He is impartial. Does that make me afraid? No. My life is secure in his hands. Christ the Judge does not question my salvation. That is settled. Rather, he requires an account of my life as a believer. Have I lived by faith? Have I embraced his commands? Have I fulfilled his purpose for my life?

That day will reveal all.

Are you ready for and looking forward to appearing before Christ Jesus?

The certainty of that day instills in me a holy reverence for you, my Lord. Thank you for your kindness and grace. Help me live responsibly so that I will have nothing to be ashamed of when I stand before you

27
TITLES

You shall be called by a new name that the mouth of the Lord will give.

Isaiah 62:2

Titles tell us about people—who they are, what they've accomplished and the things that are important to them. When describing someone, you might say, *She's a doctor,* or *a nice person,* or *he's a popular speaker,* or *a hard worker.*

Scripture also gives people titles that summarize their lives and character. But unlike the titles that we give each other, God's descriptions of us are thorough and lasting, because he sees our hearts.

Some of the titles recorded in the Bible are positive—ones we would like to have ourselves. Abraham was called "the friend of God." We know David as "a man after God's own heart." The sum of Enoch's life is that "he walked with God," and Noah was called a "righteous man."

Of course, the Bible also records some infamous titles. Tragically, Esau is said to be "godless." The notorious Ahab was found to be more evil "than all who were before him." The sad description of Solomon is that he "did not keep the Lord's command." Finally, there is the apostle Paul's words about Demas, who had forsaken him "because he loved this world."

Remembering the condition of his life before Christ, Paul said,

> For we ourselves were once foolish, disobedient, led astray, slaves to various passions and pleasures, passing our days in malice and envy, despicable, hating one another. But when the goodness and loving kindness of God our Savior appeared, he saved us, not because of any works of righteousness we had done, but according to his mercy . . . (Titus 3:3–5)

The good news is that God transforms our hearts and makes us new creations in Christ. He gives his people new names and titles. We are made righteous through the blood of Jesus Christ and called saints of God. We are fully accepted, for we are his children. Our Father also has all we need to be overcomers in this life, participating in his divine nature and escaping the corruption of the world.

What title will follow your name through eternity?

Thank you, Lord, for the hope of changed lives. You alone are able to make me a new creation, with a new nature, in Jesus Christ.

28

THE FIRST RULE OF WRESTLING

*For our struggle is not against enemies of
blood and flesh, but against the
rulers, against the authorities, against
the cosmic powers of this present
darkness, against the spiritual forces of
evil in the heavenly places.*

Ephesians 6:12

In some Scripture translations, our spiritual
struggle is called *wrestling.* Wrestling is not a
group sport, but matches one opponent
against another. When we come to know the
Lord, our ongoing wrestling match with evil
begins. We wrestle in times of sickness,
hardship or trial, as well as when we are
healthy, secure and prosperous. The Bible tells
us always to be alert, because the struggle does
not end until we leave these earthly bodies and
stand before the Lord.

In the meantime, here is a guideline to help
us persevere: *Be sure that you are not wrestling
against the Lord.* Surely we would know if we
struggled with the Lord. But, remember King
David's response after he had sinned with

Bathsheba? It wasn't until the prophet Nathan confronted him through a parable that David admitted and confessed his sin (2 Sam. 12:1–13).

Sometimes we wrestle against the Lord by resisting his word and the messengers he sends to confront us. That was true of me—although I really needed spiritual revival, initially I fought my brother's loving confrontation.

We also can wrestle with the Lord by having a spirit of ingratitude. God has promised to meet all our needs. So when we grumble about the provisions, we are grumbling against the Lord of the provision. Although we may think it is not directed at him, it is.

Once I was asked to participate in a conference in England. After flying all night, I was tired and nauseated as we drove to the campsite on the "wrong side" of the winding road. When we arrived after 10 p.m., I had to find sheets for my bed in a tiny, rustic bungalow. The electricity operated only by tokens, and I hadn't been given any. I like showers, and there was only a tub. The food wasn't good, and I like good food. After two days, I wasn't a happy camper. I was supposed to stay seven days, but the next day I told the director I wanted to go home. My excuse was "I don't think I'm communicating with the people."

He listened and said, "You can go if you want, but I wish you would stay."

Back in my little room, I got out my Bible and began to read. The Lord spoke to me, saying, *Steve you have a spirit of ingratitude. Am I not enough for you?*

That pierced my heart, and I asked God's forgiveness and thanked him for the opportunity to meet these people. Then peace came, and I knew I had to stay and minister. As it turned out, I learned things at that conference that have guided and directed me in what I'm doing today, and I also developed friendships that will last a lifetime.

Remember the first rule in the spiritual battle: *Wrestle against evil, not against God's direction and provision.*

Have you been going to the mat with the correct opponent?

Mighty Father, today I present myself to you, asking to be made righteous. I come under your authority. I take hold of every stray desire and bring every thought captive to Christ. Reign in my heart.

29

ALL HOLDS BARRED

*Instead, put on the Lord
Jesus Christ, and make no provision
for the flesh, to gratify its desires.*

Romans 13:14

Wrestlers learn to keep opponents from getting a hold on them that could lead to defeat. During the ancient Olympics, wrestlers coated their bodies with oil to protect against such holds. They trained and disciplined themselves, enduring much hardship, all to win a physical match.

But we engage in a conflict with far greater consequences—in which our spiritual well-being is at stake. The enemy of our souls is fierce and wages an attack against each of us. His tactic is to gain a hold that weakens us and gives him the upper hand.

But in Christ we have all we need to withstand Satan's attack. No matter how ferocious the assault, God provides a way of escape. When things look hopeless, don't forget that Christ is head over every power and authority and in him we are complete.

Jesus Christ lives in those of us who are

believers and breathes life into our mortal bodies. Our spirits are alive because of Christ and we no longer live to please our flesh. That sounds great, doesn't it? Yet the reality of this has to be worked out daily. We *continually* put to death the desires of our sinful nature, a process crucial to spiritual growth.

At times I have given in to temptation and allowed myself one more look, or another thought, or a little selfishness or pride. We all struggle with sinful desires, no matter how insignificant they may seem. The struggle is tiring, but giving up is dangerous! Every fall begins with a small compromise. Satan is waiting for us to give him a little room, and when we do, he pounces on our spiritual weaknesses.

Our only hope is admitting our sins to God and turning from them. With his strength (and the prayers of faithful friends) we can live godly lives for the long haul.

Have you resolved to put to death every desire and thought of your sinful nature?

Mighty Lord, you arm me for battle, providing all that I need to resist the attacks of the Evil One. By your enabling, I say no to sin and yes to all your ways.

30

TWO SIDES OF GRACE

*This gospel is bearing fruit . . . since the
day you heard it and understood
God's grace in all its truth.*

Colossians 1:6 (NIV)

I am captivated by the scriptural concept
of grace. Grace means "kindness" or "favor"
that is extended to us—not because we
deserve it, but because God loves us
immensely. Grace places us in a position of
acceptance. It is a divine gift so amazing that
it is beyond our understanding.

We are called to a balanced view of grace—
it is for us both a gift and a responsibility.
Depending on the present state of my spiritual
life I can lean toward one view or the other—
and lose my balance.

The principal song of the saints forever will
be that we are a blessed people, recipients of
God's favor through Jesus Christ. "For by
grace you have been saved through faith, and
this is not your own doing; it is the gift of
God" (Eph. 2:8). The King himself comes to
our prison cell to offer us release. Although

we are guilty of treason, he enters our dungeon and takes our place so that we can go free! No wonder the apostle Paul breaks out in spontaneous praise to God for his glorious grace: " . . . to the praise of his glorious grace that he freely bestowed on us in the Beloved" (Eph. 1:6).

I recently heard a brother speak about this grace. "I am just a sinner saved by grace," he said. "I struggle and stumble and can only hold on to the fact that his grace will cover my sin. God knows I'm only human."

I detected the sound of an excuse. Since God's grace is limitless, it will not run out. My thoughts went to the book of Romans where Paul asked, "Should we continue in sin in order that grace may abound? By no means!" (Rom. 6:1–2). God's grace never was intended as an excuse for low living. There is another side of grace.

I gently reminded my friend that the grace of God also calls for responsible action. As Scripture says,

> For the grace of God has appeared, bringing salvation to all, training us to renounce impiety and worldly passions, and in the present age to live lives that are self-controlled, upright, and godly, while

we wait for the blessed hope and the
manifestation of the glory of our great
God and Savior, Jesus Christ. He it is who
gave himself for us that he might redeem
us from all iniquity and purify for himself
a people of his own who are zealous for
good deeds. (Titus 2:11–14)

While I never cease to marvel at the gift of
salvation or tire of praising God for the grace
he has lavished on me, I must not take
advantage of it nor abuse it. Rather, his grace
enables me to respond to his high call to
purity and godliness.

*Are you balanced in your understanding of
grace as both gift and responsibility?*

*Gracious Master, I receive with reverence
your gift of salvation and your abundant grace
to live in a way that pleases you.*